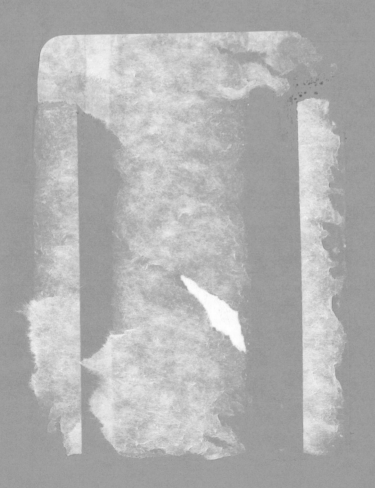

Patterns

THE MILLBROOK PRESS
Brookfield, Connecticut

Published in the United States in 1998 by

M

The Millbrook Press, Inc.
2 Old New Milford Road
Brookfield, Connecticut 06804

First published in Great Britain in 1998 by

Belitha Press Limited
London House, Great Eastern Wharf,
Parkgate Road, London SW11 4NQ

Series editor: Honor Head
Series designer: Jamie Asher
Illustrator: Kirsty Asher
U.S. Math Consultant: Henrietta Pesce

Patilla, Peter.
Fun with patterns/written by Peter Patilla; illustrated
by Kirsty Asher.
p.   cm.
Summary: Uses a variety of picture puzzles to teach
the basic geometric concept of repeating shapes to
create patterns.
ISBN 0-7613-0960–8 (lib. bdg.)
1. Geometry–Juvenile literature. 2. Symmetry–
Juvenile literature. [1. Geometry. 2 Symmetry. 3.
Shape. 4. Picture puzzles.] I. Asher, Kirsty, ill. II. Title.
QA445.5.P36 1998
510–DC21
98-16642
CIP AC

Printed in Hong Kong

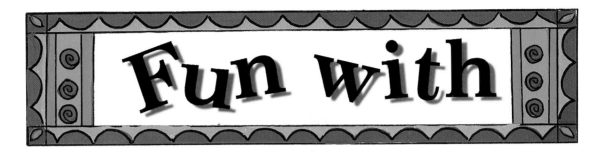

Fun with
Patterns

written by
Peter Patilla

illustrated by
Kirsty Asher

About This Series

The four books in this series, *Fun With Numbers*, *Fun With Shapes*, *Fun With Sizes*, and *Fun With Patterns*, provide an engaging format to explore beginning mathematical concepts with children. They may investigate the books on their own, but extending this investigation with an adult will bring added value to the experience. The following suggestions are provided as a guide for you to help your child or students get the most from the series.

Fun With Patterns

In mathematics, patterns are found in geometry, measurement, fractions, algebra, and computation. It is important that young children examine the concept of pattern through early experiences with simple patterns. For example, children's clothing usually has interesting patterns to explore. Talk about other patterns that are found in their environment. Ask what a child's favorite book would be like if there were no patterns in it. This might raise some interesting observations about visual patterns, language patterns, and numerical patterns. In this book, children will examine the concept of patterns, exploring both shape and color.

Before opening *Fun With Patterns*, talk about the word "pattern." What makes a pattern? What patterns can be found on the cover of the book? What shape patterns can they find? Encourage children to use language specific to geometric shapes. Talk about what the cover would look like if it were only one color. Ask why they think it is important for the illustrator to vary the color patterns. If the children are having difficulty, offer such a description yourself. As you explore the puzzles and games in *Fun With Patterns*, use these ideas to add to the mathematical journey you are about to begin.

A Step Beyond

After you have finished exploring the book, go beyond these pages. Supply the children with three or four simple shapes. Have them trace the shapes, creating a mosaic of patterns that they can color. When they have finished, display the artwork and encourage children to describe what they have created. Don't put the book away—children will want to open *Fun With Patterns* again and again.

Tent Patterns

Can you find the patterns shown
below in the picture opposite?

zigzags

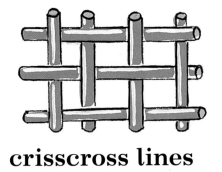

crisscross lines

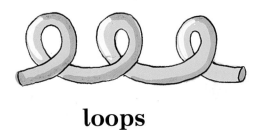

loops

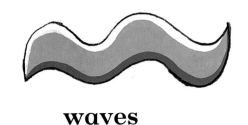

waves

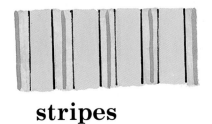

stripes

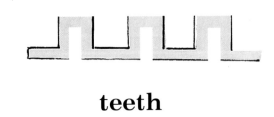

teeth

Sock Pairs

Match the socks in the drawer with the ones on the clothesline. Which socks on the line do not have mates?

9

Feathers and Eggs

Match the eggs and the peacock feathers with the same pattern.

Balls and Batons

Look at these two pictures.

Can you spot five differences?

Footprints

Match the patterns on the shoes
to the footprints opposite.

15

Flower Beds

Match these flowers to those in the picture below.

Can you find the different one in each row of flowers?

Paper Chains

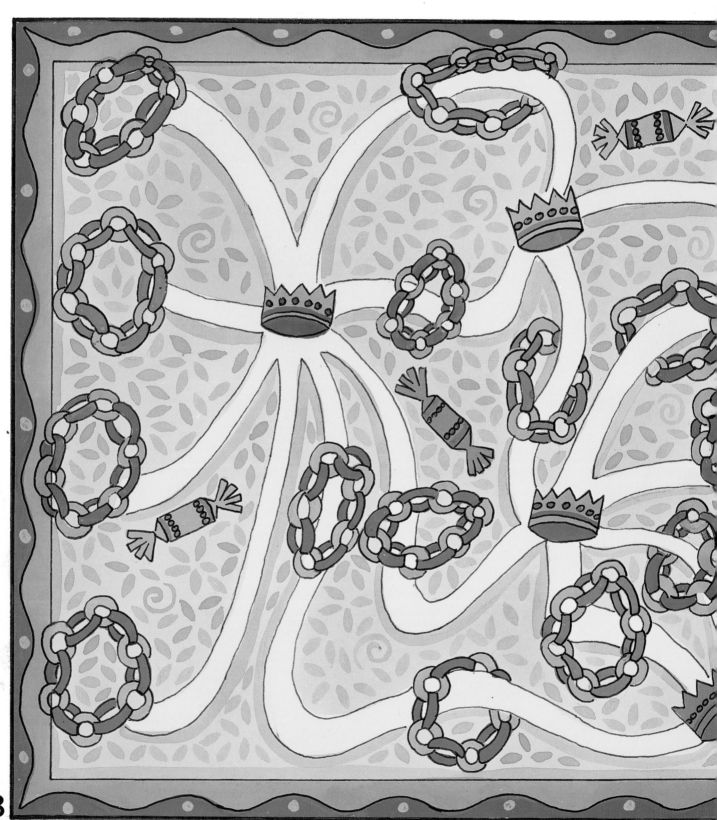

Match the paper chains at each end of the maze by following the right paths.

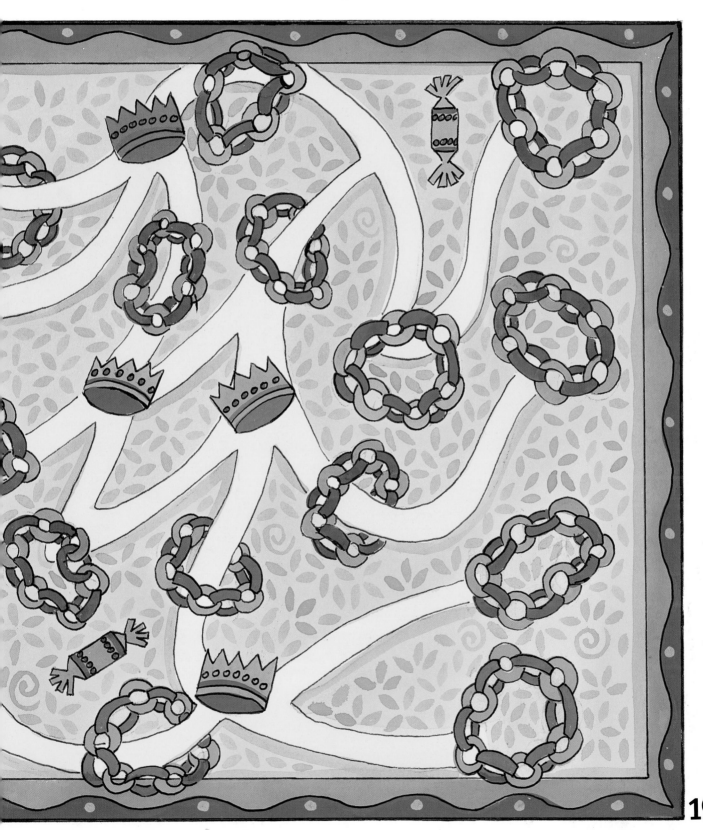

A Piece of Cake

Look at the patterns on the slices of cake below. Match them to the cakes in the picture opposite.

Towers and Flags

Some patterns are made of different shapes. Can you find the patterns below in the picture opposite?

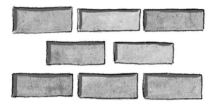

rectangles

fans

circles

hexagons

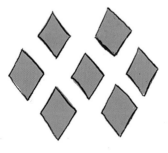

diamonds

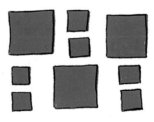

squares

Set and Match

Can you find the patterns below in the picture opposite?

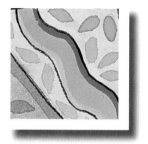

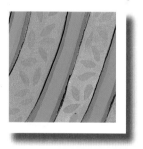

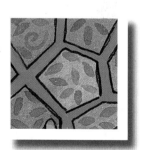

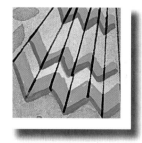

Fruits and Vegetables

Match the patterns in these fruit and vegetable pieces.

Tent Paths

Match the flags and tents by following the paths through the maze.

Falling Leaves

Find one falling leaf to match each of the trees.

Patterns

line patterns

patterns that go around

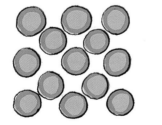 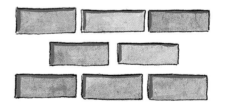

patterns made from shapes